Growing a Plant

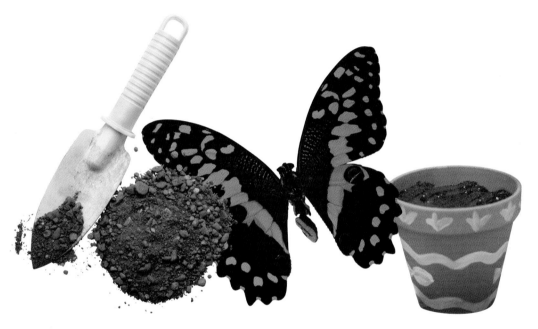

by Janine Scott

You can grow
a plant.

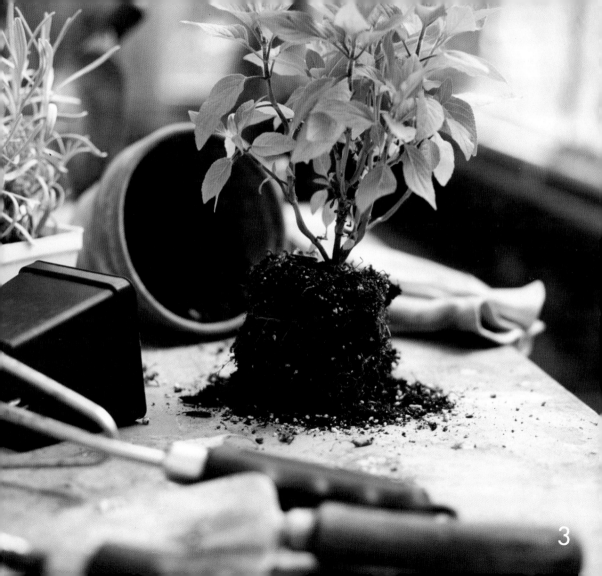

Get a pot.

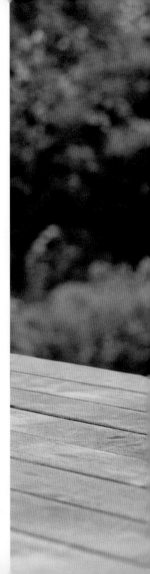

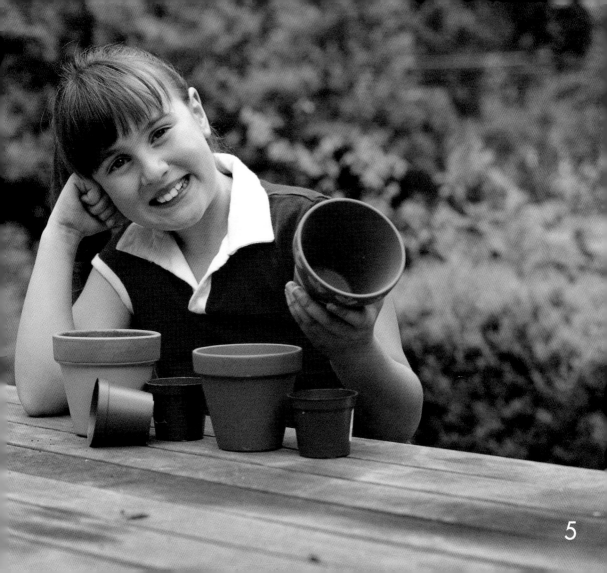

Put some soil
in the pot.

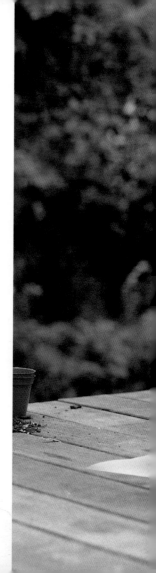

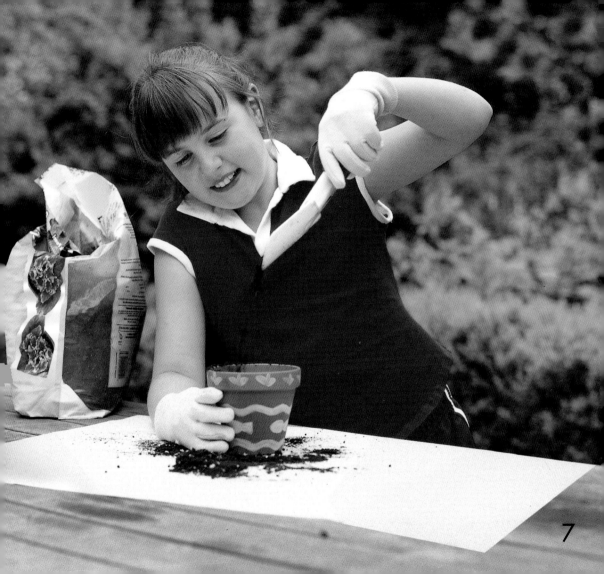

Put some seeds
in the soil.

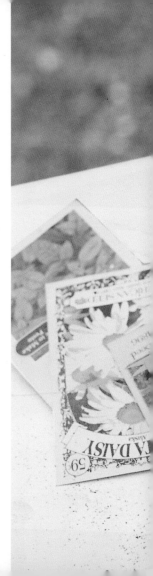

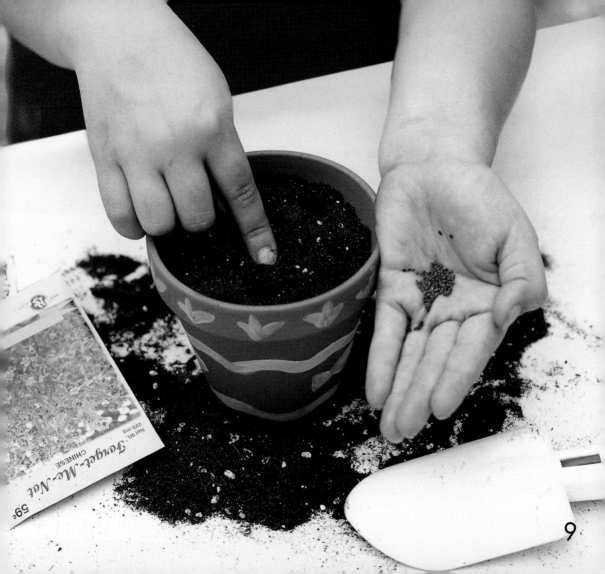

Put some water
on the seeds.

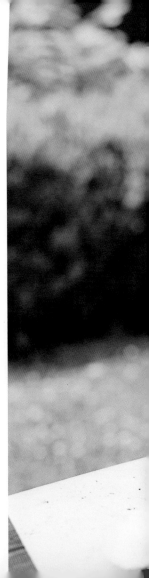

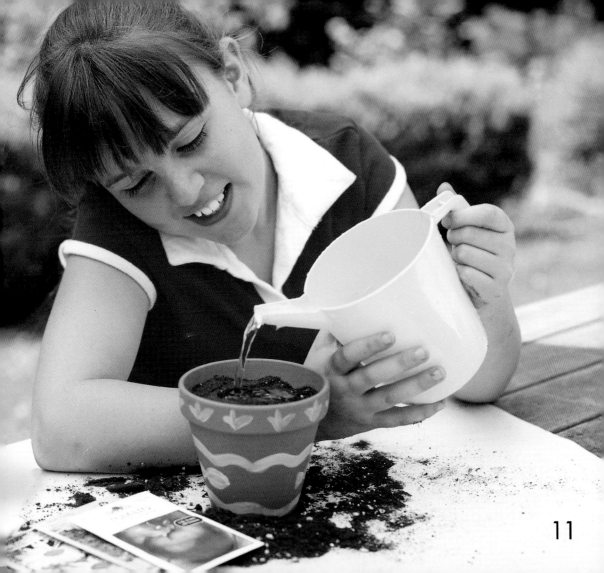

Put the pot
in the sun.

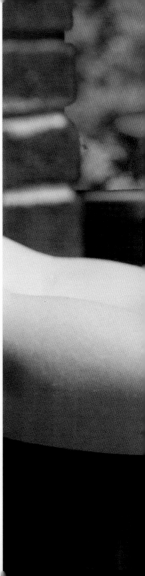

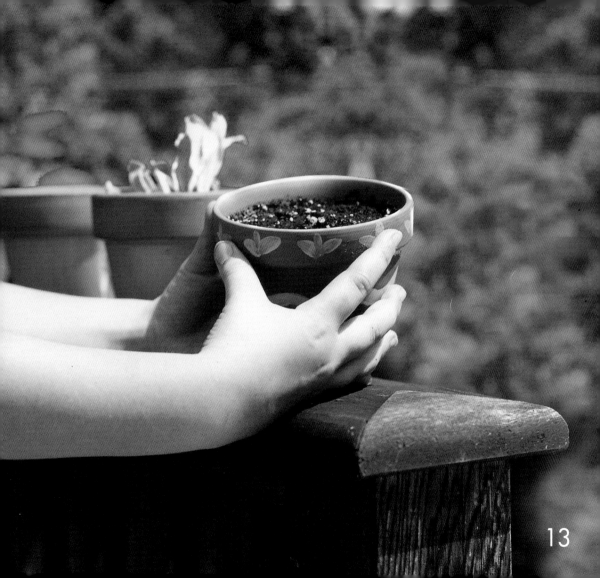

Put the plant
in the garden.

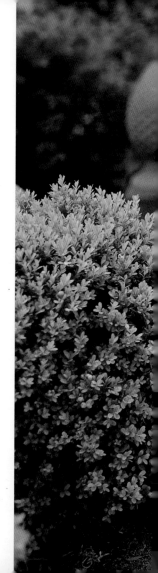

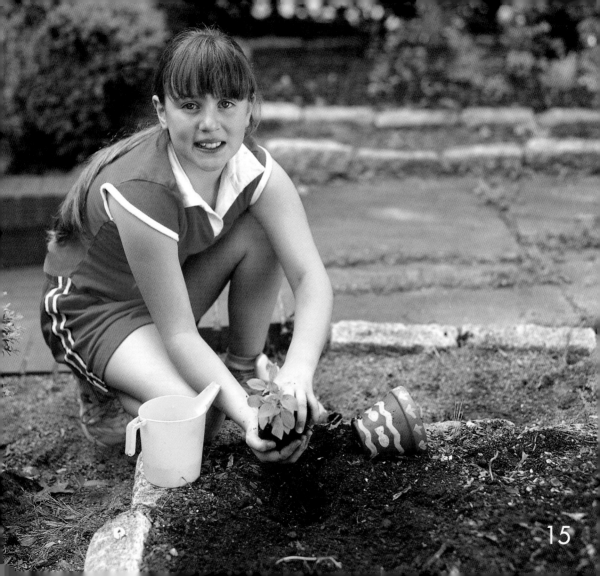

Look! The butterfly likes it.

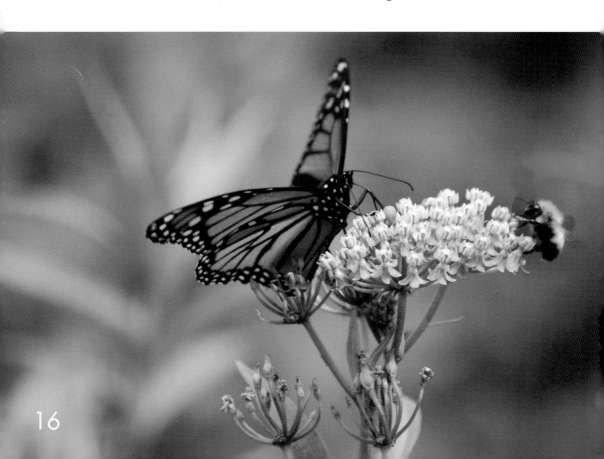